# SEA OF BROKEN MIRRORS

# SEA OF BROKEN MIRRORS

## Poems by Pablo Medina

Hanging Loose Press,
Brooklyn, New York

Published by Hanging Loose Press, PO box 150608, Brooklyn,
New York 11215. All rights reserved. No part of this book may be
reproduced without the publisher's written permission, except for brief
quotations in reviews.

www.hangingloosepress.com
Printed in the United States of America 10 9 8 7 6 5 4 3 2 1

Hanging Loose Press thanks the New York State Council on the Arts
for a grant in support of the publication of this book.

Cover art and author photo: Kassie Rubico
Design: Nanako Inoue

ISBN 978-1-934909-78-2

## Also by Pablo Medina

### Poetry

*The Foreigner's Song: New and Selected Poems*
*Soledades* (with photographs by Geandy Pavón)
*The Island Kingdom*
*Calle Habana* (with photographs by Carlos Ordóñez)
*The Man Who Wrote on Water*
*Points of Balance/Puntos de apoyo*
*Puntos de apoyo*
*The Floating Island*
*Arching into the Afterlife*
*Pork Rind and Cuban Songs*

### Fiction

*The Cuban Comedy*
*Cubop City Blues*
*The Cigar Roller*
*The Return of Felix Nogara*
*The Marks of Birth*

### Memoir

*Exiled Memories: A Cuban Childhood*

### Translation

*The Kingdom of This World* by Alejo Carpentier
*The Weight of the Island: Selected Poems of Virgilio Piñera*
*Poet in New York* by Federico García Lorca (with Mark Statman)
*Everyone Will Have to Listen* by Tania Díaz Castro (with Carolina Hospital)

*for Pablo Alejandro*

I could have been an indolent fugitive,
a clever witness of world events,
but instead I became the close friend of words,
of snow storms. Of rain.

—Sandor Csoóri,
translated from the Hungarian by Nicholas Kolumban

# Contents

# Three

# One

# CANTICLE OF THE MOON IN VERMONT

*—o graziosa luna*
Leopardi

Before the lamp is the moon
       before the moon is the map
              to the palace of time

the surrendered mottled eye
       of a seagull in a jar

mother of werewolves and hens
       trickle down sun
              caliper of clarity

moon the pox the moniker
       the biscuit dipped in milk

moon withdrawn at dawn
       moving like a Chinese bicycle
              Du Fu Li Bo Du Fu Li Bo

who has loved you cannot forage you
       give you up or turn you down

moon the enterprise
       over the gas station
              in the branches of a tamarack

used for love and used for fate
       let me kiss you luscious wafer

on the river where you shimmer
       dressed in tin and tassels
              raptured in a field of glass.

# CANTICLE OF THE POET

If the poet looked in the mirror
        he would see his ears
inflamed with the past
        he would see thin veins on his cheeks
like rivers on a distant planet
        mouth of a toad straining to catch
the poem just beyond his reach
        almost a smile almost a dance
in and out of the mirror's frame
        he will see a mockingbird
on a fence post tail flicking up and down
        before flying off into memory
he will see his sunken lips
        like an old general's
who has learned to trust defeat
        a nose that has lost its shape
sharp bone cutting air
        he will not see his tongue
or his elbows stiff and stony
        he will see the mole on his forehead
touch of the woman
        his wife would say
hair tousled thinned out
        anguish and peace
fighting a battle to the end
        on the dry bed of his intelligence
many struggles with others
        many more with himself
he will see his wife
        her closed and dreaming eyes

it was never about the money
        or the houses or the sex
he will see clouds an empty parking lot
        he wishes he could see
the island of his birth
        a storm out at sea bringing rain
water gathering in puddles
        on the road to his childhood home.

# CANTICLE OF THE MIRROR

It isn't in the mirror of today
        I see myself or yesterday
or back when I lived
        behind the funeral home
and spied the corpses
        brought in body bags late at night
or further back when
        the house cat ate her kittens
and the hurricane blew away
        the mango tree
it's in the space between time
        and memory between
the death knell and the river's
        armature called shadow
tempering the sun
        and darkening the water.


   \*         \*


My mother once told me
        she saw God walking around
the yard green and glum
        like a three-toed sloth
then she sang
        *el negrito tá en la tumba*
*y naide lo ba bucá*
        *ne ne na na ne ne na na*
a song about a black boy
        in the grave
not my kind of doom
        no one will notice or turn
his way no one torn from her sleep
        to seek him out
old love old bones
        the winding mossy way

to the end of self
        have you ever had your fate
withheld and it's the wind
        tapping your shoulder
telling you it's time?

\*        \*

Mirrors speak to one another
        and multiply
I see myself repeated
        present to past to moon's milk
dripping out of the sky
        then the murmur
of what speaks without knowing
        then the fog spreading
over the pines as spring
        swallows ambition
and the first insects awaken.

\*        \*

River high after last night's rain
        sooner than I want the day will end
and dream be real and real stamp
        its feet and clamor for the dawn
and the thrush's song
        (luck turned back at the gate)
sweet long thing sweet long running
        thing I wish I knew
how love strikes
        like the brain's refrain
river high after last night's rain.

\*        \*

The art of a blindman looking at the sky
　　　　the art of the equinox of your voice
the art of smiling at the face of death
　　　　the art of digging through the dust and clay
the art of my people the trees
　　　　the art of the stones like the eggs of time
the art of the hill's reprise
　　　　the art of knowing when to close my eyes.

# LA CAÑA DE PESCAR POEMAS

The sea means much in my poems
so do rivers and the ripples

caused by fish swimming
against the current

here in Vermont the first snow has come
and the birds have already flown south

not long ago the skies of the Everglades
darkened with flocks

and I saw on electric lines
hundreds of kingfishers

as I drove the Tamiami Trail
last winter I counted five

which has nothing to do
with poetry and a lot to do

with climate change daily now I fish
facing bare trees and sharp wind

one or two poems might come
or ideas for poems or nothing at all

then I pack up my pole
to try another spot and think

I'll write prose which is like
trying to land the big redeeming whale

soon this sun won't be so weak
and the birds that survive

will be around all year
snow a primal memory

and the Everglades a watery dream
I'll write about instead of fish.

# BIRDS UNFETTERED

Now let them roam moan
        spin around the bells of clarity
and bring with them
        the amplitude and gloss of instinct
birds have wings
        have claws have song
the monk says
        the mind is an empty vessel
we fill with fear
        eight billion humans think
they make the world eight
        billion lights and still
the darkness shines
        the monk says "In Hellblut
das Hellwort"
        in bright blood
the bright word
        this morning I cut
my finger to the bone
        out of the wound
came a stream of words
        staining the floor
the sink my clothes
        the tiniest dreams the staunchest
love cast filaments into self
        matter in thrall of energy
like the river in winter
        and death without dominion
the monk says
        "Enthusiasm is not integrity"
a boy dreams of snow
        as he dreams of sea
a man dreams
        of spring when the world
is future

and the past propellant.

\*　　　\*

      Last week a large moth
flew against the screen door,
      born too early (foot of snow
and more to come)
      I am flying
to a cold flame
      the boy sings and the man
laughs at a joke time
      played on them
in the white north
      the past blurred
*no sé por donde entra*
      *o sale la nostalgia*
*gusano roedor* don't know
      how nostalgia enters
or leaves like a gnawing worm
      that devours everything
shards remain
      where there were words
the world erases itself
      and somewhere the bright
blood is pumping
      I put my hand
under falling water
      trees of the forest comfort me
a voice calls out in the mountain
      the river makes its way to the sea.

\*　　　\*

*Via ventris*, belly road
      the monk says
"I've finally caught
      the prey I was after"

the pines cast shadows
           on the path no one
takes this far from birth
           what will I do with my doubt
and the river flows *el río fluye*
           if there is one god
there are many
           one for each thing and moment
each hammer nail
           each dereliction
a deity each time my mother
           shaved her head
or lit a cigarette or
           stared at the space she left
behind as she walked nerves in ruin
           more gods than people
more gods than gods
           in the shape of grass
the shape of water the shape
           of a dried out leaf a particle
weaving thought together
           my mother wandering
the empty rooms of the heart
           in her dance of indifference
"la maldita circunstancia
           del agua por todas partes"
the cursed condition
           of water on all sides
the sea approaches
           "this is the use of memory
liberation from the future"
           Mr. Eliot with his pants rolled up
the beginning
           is birds singing
the end is birds singing
           she among them.

# NEW PASTURES

Spring snow falling
I am walking by the river

to dispense with city air
stuck to my clothes

trapped in my hair
some vague need to embrace

whatever love has left in me
spring snow falling and the field

on the far shore glows
like the blue sheets

on which you wrote
of moves to new pastures

on that field birds now
or the memory of birds black

and scattered I think
I should run back

to where I found you
an island that insists

(as if insistence were the mirror
of existence) that water rises

every spring as the snow melts
me closer to our days together.

# CANTICLE OF THE HOUSE

I live in a house in the woods
a beautiful house of many rooms

which isn't mine my father
never lived here or my mother

or my sister or my son
in these parts my name is less

than nothing a wisp of wind
not even a thought someone had

or didn't nearby is a river full of stones
only when it floods is it a river of water

and rapids and foam once
it overflowed and came in the house

the river never belonged
to anyone though it might have

wanted to if it had a brain
and with the brain longing

and with longing regret as now
it has stones and sometimes

a lot of water flooding the yard
and the basement where I have photos

mostly black and white of my father
and mother and sister and son

who have never lived here
unlike me who has

though the river's not my river
and the house is not my house.

# CANTICLE OF THE BLACK TELEPHONE

Between the mist
        on the river and the fallen
moon on the snow
        I see myself at the edge of a field
where longing no longer blinks
        like a beach or rings like a black
telephone no one answers
        in the moment of gasping
what is its name
        the toad the catfish
what is the name of the tree
        that shadows the house
and leans ever closer to falling
        call it silver maple
call it oak or elm call it simple
        no name tree in November.


&ast;        &ast;


        The touch of the woman
in the dream is like
        the flow of water over stone
river turning green bank brown
        to the left over the road
streaks of clouds
        pines a hundred feet tall
(they sway in the wind)
        indoors the pipes are clanging
it's a long ago New York City sound
        occasionally a car
a pine cone dropping
        then a soldier keeping watch
then a comrade without arms
        then a host of faces
everyone I loved now dead
        muleteer pilot pumped-up man

meat and splash
        tendon and bone
the industry the pinnacles
        my mother waving goodbye
from her gurney my father's comb
        dropped on the hospital floor.

＊            ＊

Lord God vague you
        are the shadow of a bird
you are the boil of flesh
        the roast of thought
I am yours in the frigid north
        your will be done in the steamy south
I'm free all next week
        is that laughter
of the forest like snow
        clumping down everywhere
and greed passing for love
        mounds of garbage
politics of loam
        Lord God vague you
making me stoop to your whims.

＊            ＊

        Three trains pass one another
along the crumbling
        structures of Newark
the laughter of the brick
        the laughter of the warehouse
the laughter of the wood
        frame house leaking
into the street a muddy dog
        tied to a leaning pole barking
a purple plaster madonna
        lit by the light

of the railroad crossing
        who's to say
this lady is unhappy here
        when she lived
she saw her son flogged and crucified
        further down the line
closer to the inching trees
        a razor wire fence around a junk yard
a man bent over an engine
        salvaging a carburetor
bleat of the train
        a mound of tires
like a Matterhorn
        bleat of the train
smoke rising from a cottage in the distance
        blue and red and green
flowers on a window sill a child
without a raincoat in the rain.


\*            \*


Mother of exiles
        coming through the mist
sweet maiden could have been but not
        because God and his business partners
thought it would not be
        cost effective to keep her active
making the fields clean
        and the forests uncut and the marshes
inviting for birds and wildlife
        tenderly and despite all
his machinations
        she rose over New Jersey
for one more pass one
        more attempt to bring him down
to us at 3 AM when most people
        dream of sex and love

while a housewife of Trenton
       unable to sleep caught sight
of a fiery thing in the sky
       a semi-divine object
calling for many prayers
       and tumblers of brandy
heading like the Hindenburg
       toward the catch-all basin
of the Pine Barrens
       when hope was ascendant
and death Darwinian
       after a fine dinner of clams
and beer with the devil
       of Wildwood in a blue dress.

# THE HUMMINGBIRD

When I am healthy I sing and dance
around the fire of my ego
at night I am a lamb bleating for home
belief stands in a corner
like an invisible tree
I saw a hummingbird fly to the tallest branch
my mother lay in a bed without wings
my father prayed to the four walls
the air thickened
as the rain came in waves
in blasting wind he combed her hair
before she was wheeled away
is the hummingbird God
the smear and stain of him
in my solitude sometimes I feel
a touch hear a voice outside
my window mostly the visible trees
green come spring faith and doubt
are God and not God at the same time
when the hummingbird hovers
over the flower I remember my mother
is she here I remember my father
who never played a hand of solitaire
he believed in darkness and reason
he was master of worms he was.

# ROCK RIVER CANTICLE

I have come at last
        to the flower and the stone
*la flor y la piedra*
        and water of mountain streams
to eat the light of dusk
        bark at dying hours
and twist in bed all summer
        as the trees burst
with wise blood sap
        *sabia sangre savia*
indifferent to all save change
        from the first breeze
of the equinox
        when leaves fall one by one
to the colors
        presaging winter howls
over salt waves of snow and kernels of ice
        what voice remains
is the clack of branches
        joining overhead in rib cage
canopy I can't enter
        by memory subway
or tenderness taxi
        or fly over on magic carpet
or make my way through
        the pathways of flies
and ecstasy and bitter orange
        *amarga la naranja.*

    ✻        ✻

Once I sang of the broken
        brake downhill at en-
ervating speed
        speed of ice *hielo veloz*

*no me abandones*
       lady of the city of the rat
and the city of the brick
       and the city of the black bough
*no me abandones*
       once I was your lesser
child and now I'm not was
       a soft ball of expec-
tation looping toward home
       and now in my bones
I revel in couches
       of debauch
to cover up my crimes
       against the second person
familiar after the lights
       are out and no one listens
no one swings
       for pleasure or pines for pain
*no me abandones.*

  *　      *

       And so
I chose you to exist
       as a cross a faith a curse
you grimaced me
       and I was born you moaned
and I was expelled
       I roamed rivers in search of you
you passed indifferent
       on the street you cancelled
my ticket to the jamboree
       the outer life the life
open to wit
       dancing on the sphere of fear
bending for a daffodil
       on which malevolence
crept like an ant
       down one petal

up the next taciturn
           I move to the trees
where I can carve love messages
           before the gates of you
the metaphors
           against well-tended gardens
the unvoiced word
           the shibboleth
that opens many doors
           many heads the metal
ones and the wooden ones
           to the room of golden thoughts
and tintinnabulating bellies
           questions under answers
questions cowed by lilies
           breathing inside the stars
questions in the dark
           perplexity of your eyes.


*          *


This river where I live by day
           by night shapes
my tongue my eyelids
           inundated with love fruit
left out in the cold where I am driven
           by tenuous affection for you
and your chrysalis news of the peony
           and the cabbage
you make the path
           to my heart's content
where clouds bounce
           and eagles dally
magical water mammal
           dripping rain bolero
I go to you in search of sun
           falling leaves autumn

stains and glaze
　　　　to touch and kiss no filigrees
or arabesques just
　　　　a straight humming line
*de la piedra a la flor*
　　　　from the flower to the stone.

# Two

# THE GIFT

I am a child of the sea
but I've always lived by rivers

they're never the same
when the moon is full I stop in wonder

when winter comes I crawl in my cave
I used to love the city its buildings and clamor

now I'd rather walk in the woods
and bathe in the breath of trees

the watch on my wrist reminds me I will end
where I began time is a gift unearned

I have a dog named Diego
who hates when I leave the house

afraid I'll never return
there is no comforting him

just now he shook off
a thought he didn't like

(he learned that trick from me)
my wife sings in the morning

and tries to get me to dance
last winter we ran naked

through the falling snow
I feel blessed there are things I know

and many more I don't
my dearest friends live far away

I long for them as I long
for comfortable clothes

my son has become a man
he looks like my father

and acts like me sometimes
day will come when sleep

is a seed and the seed will grow
in ways I do not understand.

# COVID CANTICLE

The virus sallied forth in a ball
of protein and fat and I took
extra baths for protection
I was strong and beautiful
prancing through tall grass
the virus led the way the virus
was all that people talked about
not my beauty or my strength
since that was illusion and mockery
drenched in a false sense of my own
importance a misconception
of genetic substances
the virus is not self the virus
is not smart or beautiful or sad
or afraid it is pure drive being
and replication it does not like
soap or alcohol or the bloated moon
it revels in human contact a hug
a touch yesterday I saw a friend
who wore a mask from a distance
we said hello then goodbye
we embraced air we remembered
good times I walked into the mucilage
sunset if only I had washed my hands
then came the trees green this July
is the virus sexual does it rage
or miss its mother can we discuss
its rhetorical gifts as we might discuss
the Golden Age or the political ambition
of blondes it is not interested
in death or happiness
only in making many more
balls of protein and fat
just like itself a simple logic
human life will go on sadder

maybe wiser though we think
this is the end of time
nothing is the end until it comes
in a bang of dark and light
and silence sometimes I want
to drown in my shower once I lived
on a street called Virtud
virus has no eyes or stomach
no heart or brain or breath
it is a trillion trillion times itself
memorious photogenic indelible
here in Vermont the rain falls
like a curtain every day we make
coffee and bread we wait for a truce
a signal to touch again to kiss
only the stones are safe.

# CANTICLE OF WORDS AND WIND

Every day I look
in the mirror and see

a fogged-up self floating
in a sea of thighs

every day a girl comes to my table
and brings a basket of memories

my mother's watery kiss my father's ashes
buried under a lemon tree

my son chasing a goose in a long ago yard
a bird outside my window

distracts me into Spanish *mar de muslos*
I say the mirror cracks

and jags of light tangle in my hair
then comes the real poem the one

that stares me down eating words and wind
in a language that is single

and is many and is silent and is loud
the girl applauds and leaves

my table shrouded brazen
*atrevida* I say child of lullaby

and wail the one that multiplies
and the one that sits

down to die claiming defeat in the myth
of time static and time passing

when spring awakens and promises
nothing in all the languages I know.

# HOW WE LAND

*We are thrown into the world.*
                    –Heidegger

My parents had sex in a closet
in a cow pasture in the back of a bus

under an upturned boat on the beach
Cupid's arrows flew everywhere

a battle between love and reticence
some days love won some days poetry

nine months later I was born
into the screech of light and the globe of milk

the cell of infancy and babbling
the more I spoke the more my parents

clapped then the clapping stopped
and they gave me a dictionary

which dowsed me with entropy
silence my enemy dragon my fear

and the raven of prohibition
perched on my crib.

*

Nothing out of my mouth made sense
owls listened and bears growled

at least twice I tripped
and broke my head running

through the living room
or diving off the bed flight impossible.

*

Later the dog of sex bit me and I sat
rabid in my room grinding my teeth

I expected any moment the Lady of the Dream
would make an entry and tell me what to do

she never came I left the house
and hid in the chicken coop

with my lust and the clucking hens
the dog licked my face and trotted off to dinner.

*

On my own I went into the city streets
I bought some bread

I ate canned beans and ketchup
I saw two roads and took the cruder one

then quit my job and entered
the desert of penury where I found

a girl at a bus stop by a pet store
raising her hand in a wave.

# MEMORY LOSS

I am forgetting something
is it language?

I am forgetting something
my socks?

I am forgetting something
is it remembering?

everything I know
stuffed into a plastic bag

there was a trajectory
there was intent to circle back

a letter came which I read
by the window in the dimming light

memory stropped till it gleamed
memory split between

the smell of ripe guavas
and leaves burning on the snow.

# SEED OF WATER

I'm taking a chance
    before the emerald
morning waves
    let God be or be not
wind-driven I sail
    his eye from edge to edge.

The bridge of thighs
    begins at birth
it rises and descends
    and ends in tar
dead tongues I cross it
    then destroy the bridge.

My friend who prays
    and my friend who spits
kiss when the love donkey
    comes braying one wants
to ride the other wants to cheat
    the road goes all ways at once.

Do I speak-dream
    to the woods do I womb-
struggle against bliss
    sex brings a memory
a planet in a paper bag
    a puree of stamens mud lemons lies.

My blood always moves to the south
    the world of heat and rain
beyond the marshes
    where I sleep and the woman I love
is lying (her hair becomes
    the sea on her pillow).

Her hair becomes the sea
          her breath the wind and skin
the island I sail past
          on it is childhood
simmering and my mother
          singing and I tied to the mast.

# JOHN CALVIN'S SHARK

God exists and he's a gentleman in tweeds
looking down his nose at me as if I were

a creature made of oil and stink
God exists and he's a shark baring his teeth

rough hide big jaw about to pounce
while I swim across the surface of his eye

he is a vulture he is a maiden
a voyage to the country of glee

God preens himself then turns around
and asks what I've done where I've been

no one ever thanks him but in his dream
I am awake and in my dream he bites

and chews an arm a leg my heart
then comes ashore to rest on Salvation Beach.

# THE CRAB SMELL OF WINTER BEACHES

The crab smell of winter beaches
is like a politician's breath
who's been campaigning for months
without a toothbrush
he's left behind his wife his startled son
his livid lovers who thought they were the one
the politician has golden hands
blue minnow eyes a voice that grates
like the broken hinges of January
the haze of his pronouncements
turns the water gray as spoiled milk
he now chest outthrust speaks
to legions who are his mirror
man woman child a seagull
squawking in the wind
his own monument his own
neon sign advertisement.

# MORNING DOSE

Early dawn just sprung
from the woods' thin sun

birds calling out the song of things
it's not the good sense of being good

or the bad sense of being better
it's not the trumpet of triumph

or a window's dream of blue beach and seagull
not the soft air of the mountain

or the will to sail to distant corners
it's about the other side of answers

my grandmother's dentures
in a glass of water the neighbor's

mammogram's bad news
a metal rake scratching gravel

even when your game is lapidary
stone wet grave the heart's clamor

even when you claim
the morning's dose of dark laughter.

# GRANDMOTHER CANTICLE

*Mi abuela que murió de sueños.*
–Gloria Gervitz

My grandmother wore her silences
    like jewels
she threw herself at the moon
    and took her secrets
to the vegetable past
    and the electric future (choo-choo
going round the Christmas tree).

    An angel visited her
the day her husband left
    to settle the score and cackle
she migrated toward night
    with a basket of dreams on her shoulders
(whatever you do don't swallow).

    In the early morning she brought me
coffee and sang
    *éstas son las mañanitas*
*que cantaba el Rey David*
    she wanted to know why I
was writing a poem on her birthday.

    *Despierta mi bien despierta*
no one should reveal to strangers
    the mysteries of waking
that fine white sheet .
    on which I slept
those pale blue hands
    that made the bed
were her attempts to reclaim me.

# CANTICLE OF UNCLE CARLOS

Who sat with a quart bottle of cheap beer
        under the mango tree
after laying cinder blocks in the Miami heat
        all day and proclaimed
to his cousin Paco "I feel like a king."

This poem is for him
        who always felt that way
even when he was dying
        of throat cancer
and could barely speak
        through the tumor
that was choking him
        still he told dirty jokes
to fellow patients
        in the common room
and drank a beer
        I sneaked in past the nurses' station.

My father called me
        with the news
almost crying his brother
        had died and now the tree
was dying too a mere
        coincidence no doubt no doubt
we die miserably and alone
        in a nursing room
with the radio playing
        a bolero of lost love the nurses like
Uncle Carlos never took things
        seriously not money or power
not prestige or good looks
        or bad boleros
"*viva la muerte*" he said

All he ever needed was a drink
after a hard work day
        the sun shining through
the branches and his cousin Paco
        now dead as well
who marveled at the king
        on his throne under the mango tree.

# RECOLLECTION OF THE RAIN IN MIAMI

*for my mother, in memoriam*

In the afternoon came rain
in streams and spits and pings

its constant chatter trying
to be song broken by the swish

of cars outside the house
I wanted to bring the past

to her in its glory and confusion
nature's cleansing tool

against the broken motor of life
I wanted to speak to the stars

who don't know the meaning of grief
my writing not fast enough

every letter like a heavy drop
that fell before the end

and kissed her face and tasted
the amber surface of her eyes.

# POVERTY

In the darkness the depth
of your absence fills with cold water

I am a child not knowing
how to build up the fire

I pace back and forth in the living
room which means nothing

without you the wait stretches
to those blue mountains

where answers hide and wolves gather
the electric fan is clacking

I am left with coffee
in a cup without a handle.

# THE HUNT

My neighbor comes to the door
with meat from a deer he's shot

he sits on a plastic chair in the yard and tells
the story of the hunt how he went

early into the still dark cold and crouched
in the yellowing woods and waited

—You have to be willing to wait forever
to get what you want—

he pauses and whistles a tune
from long ago the *Tantum Ergo*

I heard as a child on Benediction Saturdays
—Nights he continues I spend racking myself

arguing with angels faithful and fallen alike
the next morning I walk into the woods

again and the deer may come or not
and the leaves fall all around and the trees

go bare lift their bony branches to the sky
in supplication then I hear a rustle

in the undergrowth a squirrel or a bird
maybe it's the Lord come to settle things

I fall asleep and dream of a girl frenetic
and beautiful who loved someone else

sometimes the deer appears in the dream
she lifts her head and stares her black eyes

boring into mine I raise the gun and the deer drops—
the neighbor sits back and rests

I listen to the susurrus in the breeze
—Where is the Lord now—I ask

my neighbor is getting ready to leave
—The dream and the waking come

without a sign as the Lord does
in the dark woods and in the sunlight gathering.

# Three

# UNCERTAINTY CANTICLE

Under the moon the fields
        are the color of my mother's
breast when she
        was a young woman in love
her touch like the water's
        flow over the stone
the river turning
        silver into foam
the bank brown slate
        sky mottled
into yellow husk
        across the road the pines
sway like the earth's bones
        this was my last
experiment in solitude
        by the river in the woods
what I did
        what I failed to do
I returned to the city of birth
        a curl in lost time
slowly pablo suddenly sane.

     \*       \*

The river is long soup
        unchartable as your voice
high sometimes
        fast and churning
or dense and slow as your foot
        making its way up my thigh
how can full be empty
        and empty full
nothing is more certain
        than uncertainty

I saw you thin I saw you
          clean I fell in love
decked out pushed out
          street angel left for dead
I curried favor not with kings
          but with the kinks and flings
of sameness and dissent
          I went at night
to the streets of bored hordes
          the painted women
sniffing powder with smeared men
          I made it home
before dawn with torn shirt
          stained pants and twenty
cents in my pocket
          if you spend
don't spend halfway
          if you make mistakes
let them come in waves
          cookie trays champagne
glasses music boxes
          unmade beds
over the water
          the mist gathers slowly
the sun breaks like an egg
          and spills through the woods
a black telephone rings
          no one answers
the lamb is brought to the sacrifice
          the festival ends in the sea.

# RAIN DELAY IN BOSTON

I love the way umbrellas
move up and down past my window

and dogs lead their owners
helter-skelter from one wet tree to another

day it thunders sky breaks
and beats down rain moves taps squeals

from the street to the avenue from a childhood
memory to the hay of a cane field

puddles become streams
streams run to the sea day it rains

a fire dies inside the water
clears the way to the forest of forever.

# AFTER MY FATHER'S CREMATION

Outside now his ashes
are blown by the wind

through the eyes of ten needles
he was the poorest man

he was the richest man
he floats with one ear on the horizon

and listens to the siren song of the flames
too late to make excuses

his tongue tastes the skin of the sea
his lips are the waves breaking on the beach.

# THE BUTTERFLY EFFECT

This city is a psalm of plenty
cocoons dangle from the bridge

butterflies hatch and fly
across the river to New Jersey

butterflies I said through layers
of light and my best intentions

the lack of splendor has devoured them
here on the corner someone

left a torn pantyhose a crumpled love
note a chicken bone this city

with a tunnel's mouth
a siren's voice the heart

of a subway mendicant
this city begging for God's mercy.

# CUBOP CITY CANTICLE

At first I wandered the streets
        of Manhattan
till my feet gave out and my mind
        sprang loose by Grant's tomb
I looked across the river
        to New Jersey and heard
the Catholic bells
        (clang and taint of faith)
ate mangoes
        in East Harlem a pizza slice
on 14th Street
        (oh universal wedge of taste)
and found the kindling
        of a fire about to burst
from the heart of the new order.

   *        *

At the bus stop some days
        other days caught
in the headlights
        of a dump truck
I tried to decipher myself
        in Spanish English or both
*quizás no tenga amor la eternidad*
        that old bolero
eternity doesn't wait for anyone
        eternity has nothing
to do with language
        anonymous odorous hordes
passed by me and I too
        was anonymous sweaty
Cubop City was new land then
        long on arteries

short on blood
       I faced a weak sun
in the morning a wan moon
       at night I heard the subway's
rattling roar
       the honk of taxis
impatient yellow geese
       the city reveled in straight lines
and glass panes the liberal application
       of concrete and steel
smeared bagel for breakfast
       bitter coffee from the corner cart.

   *       *

Cubop City is like a novel
       spreading outward from a point
where you happen to find yourself
       when the lights go on
a café where the night hawks
       are fueling their insomnia
a street corner where a man gets knifed
       while people go about their lives
and hope that from their constancy
       comes the antidote
against the claims of time.

   *       *

In the afternoon I walk
       with the warmth of the sun at my back
the street alive with grand dames
       politicians drivers of armored trucks
cooks waiters tax collectors
       yoga teachers strip teasers
goth teenagers and I bilingual
       loafer among them
I remember the past
       about to end

the sound of breaking waves
        the taste of tamarind I remember
an island between two rivers
        a garland around the bay
the organism that took my childhood
        away and gave me the gift
of manhood I will know nothing
        like I know this city
rock-hewn crystallizing
        into which I disappear.

# MASQUERADE CANTICLE

On the night of the party
      one neighbor arrives naked
another wears a pink armor
      a scowl on his face
three women show up as my wives
      they bicker first then join
in a war dance
      around a fire in the living room
they throw cinders at me
      I run and hide behind the drapes
disguised as myself
      in a suit of innocence
Rachel La Cubana sways
      across the living room
and gives me a look
      that says *noli me tangere*
Tongolele shakes her hips
      while drinking a daiquiri
one character I've never met sings
      the national anthem swings a bat
and breaks Aladdin's lamp
      no genie appears
but smoke fills the room
      and my three wives
convince Victor Mature
      (the sorrowful eyes the tight muscles
the glittering curls)
      to pin me to the wall
while they throttle me
      with my own belt
my pants around my ankles
      death is a fantasy I use
to fool my enemies.

     ✻        ✻

I expected the card sharp
        to save me
with his legerdemain and devil-may-care
        tricks but he went home
with the bearded lady
        I'm wearing a moribund mask
which frees me from eating
        sleeping and washing
the longer I wear it
        the more it suits me
is this a poem
        I'm writing or a story floating
in a willing suspension of jelly fish
        disbelief is a cynic's disguise
a plinth a pope a *Weltanschauung*
        ask Diogenes
who came as a dog
        and urinated on the rug
I threw him out
        on the busy street
what matters is
        I've moved on
I'm a snake devouring its tail
        a toilet bowl from which
a rosebush grows
        replicating the Sphinx
If you want me you will find me
        with the worms
postulating entropy
        in the spiritless world.

# THE WATERS OF THE MIND

The day goes from hot to cold to hot
again a woman becomes a deer

two old people become trees
locking branches overhead

the second coming is at hand
and the hand is a spider the spider

is a monkey swinging from bough
to bough leaves wither and die

they cannot help themselves ideas
become things things become ideas even

you turn into a great blue heron hungry
in midflight who sees a frog plop into a pond.

# DROWNING DOG
*after Goya*

To drown in an ochre sea is to find
the molten sun at the end of time
*bark bark* the dog thinks or whimpers
tries to stay afloat above the wave
about to break on a bad day
when canine afterlife is at stake
but never sanctioned (like belief).

Deaf the man who painted him
deaf his house his canvasses the dog
swimming up the curl of his poise
his effort to rise to the yellow
smoke of salvation in God's eye
a faint command to swim for life
before the wave crashes and he drowns.

# MELANCHOLY BABY

Every New Year's Eve is the same
I build things up I eat bad food

I drink champagne which I don't like
and then I kiss and kiss and wish and wish

and nothing comes next day
I rummage through the house

and find the manifest of the ship of my destiny
all the passengers are gone or about to go

if I write the words are clumsy
before the desert sea ahead

if I read I'm soon bored and fall asleep
I wish I had a pet I could feed or stroke

but my last pet died upside down of neglect
so have all the plants I've ever owned

I live with silverfish who eat my books
plenty of food here till I die probably

on the couch waiting while my friends
outside bang the door and sing

Melancholy Baby and dance away the stars.

# HOME ALERT GHAZAL

The place you're in defers to a curving road
and a translation announces you aren't home

*pan* is not bread *nariz* is not nose
*pez* is not fish language is your only home

your share of emotional quotients
paints a myriad versions of memory's home

love and betrayal cancel the dunes
where the river meets the sea away from home

a boat adrift in the swelling waves means
no roots means no sap means no home

tranquility made a name of silence
childhood exists only at home

dishwasher loaded classical music playing
wild flowers bundled as if this were home

yesterday soup and crackers tonight the moon
darkness is no place like home

Poet arise and listen to the cricket's song
in the templates of hope the ruins of home.

# KASSIE IN THE GARDEN

Kassie's in the garden
planting the flowers
that bless us
unaware she is the flower
with a prickly
stem that draws blood
blood I said
look at those petals
red and succulent
Lucifer time Lucifer
and God dancing a sardana
sweating out the many
poisons of life
when she's done
she comes back in
and drinks a glass of water

she's taking a shower now.

# NOTES TO MYSELF

*Quien habla solo espera hablar a Dios un día.*
—Antonio Machado

The man who took away your country
liberated you

you found it again by the Hudson River

what you cannot remedy
you cannot forget

the bengal tiger the dodo bird

*río de no volver*

the sea is full of broken mirrors

reading clouds reading books

*a veces en español a veces en inglés*

get used to not belonging

a blackbird on the snow

you'll never abandon what calls you away

*hay caminos que nacen de los cantos*
*y cantos que nacen de los caminos*

a moth stuck on the window screen
fire spreads to the end of night

*lluvia de cenizas desde el bus*
*como si fuera el fin del mundo*

do not fear your last breath
fear the one that follows

what if the soul dies as the body dies

yesterday does not exist nor tomorrow

think about the meal you will prepare your lover
her favorite ingredients

*mi abuela desplumando un pollo*

a leaping frog doesn't know
where it will land

a human doesn't know
 any more than a frog

*la vida es sueño* then

sleep as if you were dead
always dreaming.

# LAST BUS

Last bus comes at ten pm
after that is anybody's guess

I am standing by a pet shop
watching fish swim back and forth

some are languid some invisible
a small fish comes close

to my nose and nibbles (ouch)
the larger ones are out

on the hunger highway
I wait therefore I think

all song all hope
cantilevered into space.

# Acknowledgments

My gratitude to the following periodicals where these poems first
 appeared:

"Rain Delay in Boston" *Analog Sea*
"Morning Dose" (as "Dark Matter") *Barrow Street*
"Canticle of the Mirror" *Copper Nickel*
"La caña de pescar poemas" (as "Climate Change Canticle") and
 "Melancholy Baby" *Hanging Loose.*
"After My Father's Cremation" *The New Yorker.*
"Canticle of Uncle Carlos" and "Uncertainty Canticle (as "New
 Order Canticle") *On the Seawall*
"The Crab Smell of Winter Beaches" *PEN America Website*
"The Gift" *Ploughshares*
"The Hunt" (as "*Canticle of the Deer*") *Presence*
"How We Land" *Salt*
"Home Alert Ghazal" and "Canticle of the Poet" *Zyzzyva*


Fred Arroyo, Gregory Orfalea, Kassie Rubico, John Skoyles, and
 Mark Statman read the manuscript or parts of the manuscript
 and offered comments and suggestions that enriched and
 emboldened its contents.

I am indebted to Hanging Loose Press and the editors there, Jiwon
 Choi, Joanna Fuhrman, Caroline Hagood, Dick Lourie, and
 Mark Pawlak, their friendship and their sharp editorial sense;
 art editor Elizabeth Hershon worked overtime to listen to my
 ideas and get the cover just right.

I am grateful as well to friends and family whose presence along
 the way has illuminated my meandering path. Among them are
 Arístides Falcón-Paradí, Isabel Alvarez-Borland, Iraida Iturralde,
 Lourdes Gil (in memoriam), Adriana Méndez Rodena, Sergio
 Díaz Briquets, Rolando Bonachea, Dan Aubrey, Jim Earp,
 Enrique del Risco, Pamela Painter, Kate Painter, Christine
 Triebert, Carol Ross, Airea D. Matthews, Rodney Jones,

Eleanor Wilner, Alberto Vadía, Peter Eliopoulos, Jerald Walker, Emily and Kristina Rubico, Brittany Burgess, my sister Silvia Poprovak Medina, my agent Duvall Osteen, and my partner Kassie Rubico, who keeps me grounded, digging and smiling much of the time.

# Notes on the Poems

## Canticle of the Mirror

- *"El negrito tá en la tumba y naide lo ba bucá."* An apocryphal lullaby. "The black boy is in the grave/and no one goes to look for him." My mother learned it from her mother. I've never heard anyone else sing it.

- *"La caña de pescar poemas"* — The phrase can be awkwardly rendered as "The poetry fishing pole."

## Birds Unfettered

- *"In Hellblut das Hellwort."* Paul Celan. "In bright blood the bright word."

- "Enthusiasm is not integrity." Kenneth Rexroth.

- *"No sé por dónde entra/o sale la nostalgia gusano roedor."* — "I don't know where nostalgia enters or leaves like a gnawing worm."

- *"Via ventris,"* from the Latin, meaning belly road.

- "I've finally caught the prey I was after, " Ovid, *The Art of Love*, Book Two.

- *"El río fluye."* — The river flows.

- *"La maldita circunstancia del agua por todas partes. "* — "The cursed condition of water on all sides." Virgilio Piñera, "The Weight of the Island."

- "This is the use of memory/liberation from the future." T.S. Eliot, "Four Quartets."

## Rock River Canticle

- *"Hielo veloz"* — Fast ice.

- *"No me abandones"* is a free translation of Jacques Brel's *"Ne me quitte pas."*

- *"De la piedra a la flor"* — From the stone to the flower.

## Canticle of Words and Wind
- *"Mar de muslos"* — sea of thighs
- *"Atrevida"* — bold or brazen.

### Grandmother Canticle

- *"Estas son las mañanitas que cantaba el rey David"* and *"Despierta, mi bien, despierta"* are lyrics from *"Las mañanitas,"* a popular birthday song in Mexico.

### Canticle of Uncle Carlos

- *"Viva la muerte"* — "Long live death." It also happened to be the battle cry of the Spanish phalangists during the Spanish Civil War.

### The Hunt

- *"Tantum Ergo"* — A hymn attributed to Thomas Aquinas, sung in Latin in the adoration ceremonies of the Roman Catholic Church before the reforms of the 2nd Vatican Council.

### Cubop City Canticle

- *Cubop City* is the title of a composition by Mario Bauzá.
- *"Quizás no tenga amor la eternidad"* are lyrics from the bolero *"Sabor a mí"* by the Mexican composer Álvaro Carrillo.

### Masquerade Canticle

- Rachel la cubana was a courtesan in 1920s Havana.
- *"Noli me tangere"* is from the Latin for "Don't touch me," a phrase spoken by Jesus to Mary Magdalene after the resurrection.
- Tongolele (Yolanda Montés) was a famous rumba dancer and actress active from the late 1940s to 1980.

### Home Alert Ghazal

- *Pan* — bread.
- *Nariz* — nose.
- *Pez* — fish.

## Notes to Myself

- "*Río de no volver*" —River of no return.

- "*A veces en español, a veces en inglés.*" — At times in Spanish, at times in English.

- "*Hay caminos que nacen de los cantos y cantos que nacen de los caminos.*" —There are roads that are born from songs and songs that are born from roads.

- "*Lluvia de cenizas desde el bus como si fuera el fin del mundo.*" —Rain of ashes from the bus as if it were the end of the world.

- "*Mi abuela desplumando un pollo.*" —My grandmother plucking a chicken.

- "*La vida es sueño.*" The title of a play by Pedro Calderón de la Barca (1600–1681).